AQUAPONICS

101

The Easy Beginner's Guide to
Aquaponic Gardening: How To Build
Your Own Backyard Aquaponics
System and Grow Organic Vegetables
With Hydroponics And Fish

Tommy Rosenthal

REVIEWS

Reviews and feedback help improve this book and the author.

If you enjoy this book, we would greatly appreciate it if you were able to take a few moments to share your opinion and post a review on Amazon.

Table of Contents

Introduction

Thank you for picking up this copy of '***Aquaponics***
101*: The Easy Beginner's Guide to Aquaponic*
Gardening: How To Build Your Own Backyard
Aquaponics System and Grow Organic Vegetables
With Hydroponics And Fish'!

What is aquaponics?

Aquaponics is a system that combines aquaculture
(where you raise fish) and hydroponics (where you
grow plants without soil). The plants get their organic
nutrients from the waste produced by the fish. In turn,
the plants purify the water. This creates a healthy
ecosystem for both the plants in fish.

Deciding to start your own aquaponics systems is a
step closer to providing you with a wealth of benefits
for a number of areas in your life. The decision can be
made for a number of reasons and these are unique to

you. For example, you may have decided to research further into aquaponics and designing your own system for the purpose of growing your own food such as fruits, vegetables and fish.

You may have made the decision to explore into more sustainable methods of growing plants without consuming too many resources such as water and electricity.

Perhaps you are searching for a new hobby that involves getting out in the garden and you feel that traditional forms of gardening are not for you.

Whichever the reason, you will discover through this book that aquaponics is an exciting interest that has many benefits to enrich your life and provide you with plenty of enjoyment along the way.

Getting started in aquaponics requires very little skill and knowledge. Most of which you will discover through reading this book. The resources that you will need to get started can be found in hardware and gardening stores in your local area and are quite inexpensive. In fact, you will soon discover that aquaponics is one of the most cost-effective ways to grow your plants without consuming too much water, electricity and fertilizer as the system is quite self-sufficient.

At the completion of this book, you will have a good understanding of:

- the benefits that aquaponics can bring you, and
- the reasons behind why it is fast becoming more popular for farmers, particularly in areas that are prone to droughts and where sourcing water is difficult.

In the first chapter, we will explore the advantages aquaponics has over traditional forms of gardening as well as hydroponics. We will also look into the definition of aquaponics, what the process involves, and how it all ties together.

In the second chapter, we will look into the various systems and setups you can have for aquaponics, as well as the advantages and disadvantages of each one and the types of plants that suitable for each type of setup.

In the third chapter, we will use an example system to walk through the process of designing your own aquaponics backyard system, and the materials that you require.

The fourth chapter will explore the various types of fish and plant life that are recommended for your tank. It will also detail the suitability of your tank in terms of the climate and the accompanying plants that can be grown in similar water temperatures.

The fifth chapter will take a look at the maintenance of your tank, and the small actions required frequently to keep your tank running at optimal efficiency and to prevent any failures that could result in expensive repairs.

The sixth and final chapter will look into the various locational aspects you will need to take into account when you are finding a space for your system, particularly what to avoid and what will be best for your system.

Aquaponics is a wonderful way of growing your own organic fruit and vegetables. This book will teach you everything you need to know. So, I hope you are excited, let's get started with the basics of Aquaponics!

Chapter One: What is Aquaponics?

Key Takeaway: Aquaponics, the combination of aquaculture and hydroponics, is changing the face of farming and the growing of vegetables. It can be achieved by anyone willing to learn and has great benefits far outstripping those of regular gardening and hydroponics.

Defining Aquaponics

There aren't too many practices that, when combined, can expand on the advantages of each other while reducing and in some cases eliminating the limitations of each. Aquaponics can be thought of this way. For this reason, it will truly bring your garden to life in more ways than one. You may be thinking what exactly is Aquaponics, though it is really quite simple yet ingenious.

Aquaponics, to put it simply, is the coming together of aquaculture (the raising of fish) and hydroponics (growing plants without the need for soil). This ultimately creates one integrated system that provides food and nutrients for fish who in turn create waste that, through microbes and worms that thrive amongst the environment, convert that waste into fertilizer for the plants to allow them to continue providing the fish with an abundant environment.

This occurs as the microbes or nitrifying bacteria and red worms convert ammonia from the fish waste into nitrates, as well as the solids into vermicomposting, creating a viable food source for the plants.

If you would like to learn more about Hydroponics, check out my book *'Hydroponics 101: The Easy Beginner's Guide to Hydroponic Gardening. Learn*

How To Build a Backyard Hydroponics System for Homegrown Organic Fruit, Herbs and Vegetables.'

Back to Aquaponics.

There are three methods used to establish your aquaponics system: media based, raft based and a hybrid combination of these two.

1. **Media Based** – The name comes from the media (gravel, clay, pellets and other material) in which the plants are grown. The media allows for the ammonia based waste and mechanical waste to filter through. This means there is less work to do to maintain the system. The media based system is often more suited towards growing larger plants that provide fruit.

2. **Raft Based** – The raft based system makes use of a foam raft that floats in a channel accessible to the filtered fish effluent water. The plants are secured in holes along the raft, while the roots have access to the water below. The raft based

method is suitable for growing smaller plants, such as salad greens and other plants that require less nutrients to thrive.

3. **Hybrid Method** – Using a combination of the two, the media beds are able to filter the solid waste prior to the water entering the raft system. This is ideal as it provides further flexibility in the planting process and means much lower maintenance. While this system may be more expensive to establish, the benefits allow you to have a wider range of what you grow in your garden and a much higher yield.

Advantages Over Traditional Gardening

Soil based gardening not only takes additional effort and maintenance, the practice is rife with drawbacks that leave your garden a constant source of attention without providing a reliable return. Traditional gardening through the use of soil requires constant watering, particularly in hotter climates. This will take effort on the part of the individual who has to water the garden, either yourself or a paid gardener, or an irrigation system, which can be quite costly to both establish and use. This doesn't take into account the fact that you will need to constantly monitor your garden for weeds which can crop up over time, draining precious resources and nutrients from the plants you had placed so much effort in providing an environment in which they are able to thrive.

Then comes the insects that live amongst the soil. Going out to admire your garden can come with a shock when you discover that your plants are under attack from a pest that is slowly destroying them. These pests are not just limited to insects, they can come in all shapes, sizes and species. Think rabbits, raccoons, or anything else that finds its way into your garden to feast on your hard work.

While some people enjoy the time they spend working their garden, it is not always best for your health. The more effort you extend towards your garden, the more strain you may be placing on your body such as your back, knees, hands as well as the additional risk of being exposed to the sun. Over time, and as you maintain your garden, this damage can become significantly noticeable. However, this is all avoidable with aquaponics.

If you feel as though aquaponics may have some learning curves to overcome or that establishing your system may be more complex than you had originally thought, this is no truer than the case for traditional methods of soil gardening. With traditional gardening, you need to learn the correct timing for:

- when to water your garden
- how much is required
- the fertilizers to use, and
- what soil composition you need for which plants.

How Does Aquaponics Differ From Hydroponics?

You might be thinking that these issues can be overcome with traditional hydroponics, the growing of plants without the need for soil. Traditional hydroponic systems can be quite costly and require additional chemicals, sales and other trace elements to create the right environment for the plants you are growing.

These mixtures also need to be carefully analyzed to ensure that the correct pH level is adhered through the use of additional meters and tools. On top of this, the water in your hydroponic system require replacement frequently due to the buildup of sales and chemicals which become toxic to the plants that rely on them. This presents an entirely separate issue on its own, the disposal of this mixture needs to be environmental considerate.

Even more alarming, hydroponic systems are prone to a disease which can be devastating to your plant life.

The disease is known as "Pythium", or root rot. While it can found in traditional hydroponic systems, it is extremely rare in aquaponics.

The case for aquaponics is that your fish can be fed anything from just standard inexpensive fish food all the way to food scraps from the house that you want to dispose of. This means you have a reliable system for composting that doesn't require additional harmful chemicals and salts.

The monitoring of your aquaponics system consists of nothing more than testing the pH and ammonia levels on a weekly basis and of course if there are any visible issues with the fish in the system or the plant life. It is advised that you keep an eye on your system during the initial month or so to ensure that operations are running smoothly. This also provides an opportunity to correct any issues before they destabilize the system down the track.

The water system in your aquaponics set up doesn't require any discharging or replacing. The only reason it would ever need to maintained is during hotter months or when the water evaporates naturally in which case you will only need to provide a top up to keep the fish and plant life content.

Why Aquaponics is Relevant Today

As our society moves towards more renewable and sustainable methods of growing food, the concept of Aquaponics was developed through research established in the 1970s spearheaded by Dr. James Rakocy at the University of the Virgin Islands. It was developed as a means of finding a way for plants to act as a natural filter. From here, the benefits of aquaponics became evident, as it further evolved in the 1980s and 1990s, to establish the systems as we understand them today.

Aquaponics solves many of the previous drawbacks of traditional gardening as well as hydroponics. The reduction in waste has been an advantageous feature for farmers looking for a way to conserve their water resources while also having an environment to breed fish. Aquaponics is noted to only use around 10 percent of the water that similar setups in soil based gardening use, and even less than that of hydroponics. This more efficient use of resources is also evident considering that the set up relies on a consistent abundance of water. This means you can never underwater or overwater the plants. The same can be said for the availability of nutrients, meaning your system no longer requires consistent fertilization.

The toxic by-product of the chemicals used in previous systems was detrimental to the environment and unsustainable in the long run, particularly for larger scale operations. Aquaponics focuses on natural resources and by-products of the fish to provide all the nutrients required to keep the plants health and stable in their growth.

The time and effort used to maintain an aquaponics system is a stark contrast with other more traditional methods. Rather than straining the body, using precious and limited resources, you are able to focus on tasks such as feeding the fish and tending to and harvesting your plants.

In recent years, aquaponics has become an increased focus in commercial farming with a number of associations and communities being established to represent aquaponics in the farming industry such as the Aquaponics Association. The mission behind the association was to promote aquaponics and to continue the progress of the technology to support the systems for further growth and development through annual conferences, attracting practitioners of aquaponics from around the world.

Chapter 2: The Different Aquaponics Systems Explained

Key Takeaway: There are many components of an aquaponics system, each with its own unique function as well as many suitable set ups that each their own advantages and disadvantages. Decide on a setup that works for you, based on the resources you have available and the vegetables you will be growing.

Due to the dual nature of the aquaponics system, the system itself consists of two primary parts. These are:

- The aquaculture system, which is dedicated towards raising the aquatic creatures or and
- the hydroponics system which is dedicated in growing the plants.

The system is designed to be self-sufficient, with each part of complimenting and maintaining the other.

The aquatic effluents, which are a by-product of either the food scraps you provide to the fish or from the fish themselves, build up in the water. This would normally become harmful to the aquatic life, particularly if there is no recirculation of the water as is the case for our system. This is where the advantages of aquaponics come into being, the effluent waters, while toxic without any intervention, becomes fuel for the plant life due to the high concentration of nutrients.

As we take a greater look at our system, we are able to break down the two main functions of the system into the components or subsystems which work together to provide food for the plants and keep the fish healthy in their environment.

Components

Rearing Tank

The rearing tank is built as a home for the fish. This is where they both live, breed and feed.

Settling Basin

The settling basis is a unit for catching the uneaten food, biofilms which have become detached, and for settling out fine particulates.

Sump

The sump is the portion of the system where the water descends to the lowest point, allowing it to be pumped back into the rearing tanks to start the entire process again.

Biofilter

The biofilter is where the plants collect their nutrients. It is where the nitrification bacteria grow and accumulate for the conversion of the ammonia, created by the fish into nitrates to act as fuel for the plants.

Hydroponics Subsystem

The hydroponics subsystem is the area where plants are grown and fed through the water, allowing them to collect the excess nutrients which is passed through. This system is similar to a traditional hydroponics setup in that the roots are immersed in the water which is comprised of nutrients and effluent focused towards providing the plants with powerful resources to grow as opposed to using soil or fertilizer. The hydroponics system itself can be constructed in a variety of set ups:

Deep Water Raft Aquaponics: This makes use of styrofoam rafts, which are suspended in a deep aquaculture basis in troughs.

Recirculating Aquaponics: The use of solid media such as gravel or clay beads are stored in a container which is then filled with water from the aqua culture. This type of aquaponics has also been referred to as closed-loop aquaponics.

Reciprocating Aquaponics: This system uses solid media in a container, which is then flooded before being drained making use of a number of different siphon drains. This process has also become known as flood-and-drain as well as ebb-and-flow aquaponics, due to its nature.

Nutrient Film Technique Channels: As the name implies, long narrow channels are used to house the plants and allow a film of nutrient rich water to move through these channels, making contact with the plants roots along their journey. Due to the fact that there is a limited amount of water flowing through such small channels, bacteria integral to the process are unable to survive in the environment. Therefore, a bio filter is necessary.

The Process

There are a number of methods you can use to have your system up and running, each having its own advantages and disadvantages. It is important to select a system that you feel comfortable with and takes into account:

- your budget
- the plants you would like to grow
- the level of maintenance you will be undertaking
- the type of fish you will be stocking, and
- the equipment you have available. The

The methods for running a system are the following.

Chift Pist

If you are putting together your own system, the Chift Pist is a popular one for many people. The water for the main fish tank is pumped through the sump tank and this in turn fills the fish tank, until it starts to flow into the grow bed. The nutrient rich water is then dispersed throughout the grow bed, before being finally drained back into the sump tank to be reused once again. The process can sometimes employ an auto siphon within the grow bed to ensure it is drained. Or it can be drained periodically as the grow bed is constantly flooded.

It is also recommended that you incorporate an SLO (Solids Lift Overflow) into the system. This will allow the overflow pip in the fish tank to have access to the base of the tank, to bring any solids that have been deposited on along the bottom and distribute them back into the grow bed.

The advantage of having this type of system is that the water level in the fish tank remains at its constant maximum, keeping the fish content. This system works well if you have a tall fish tank, as it also allows for a much larger water volume due to the sump.

The disadvantages with this type of system is that you do require the extra sump tank, as well as the taller fish tank if you don't already have one. It can also use up more resources.

Simple Flood and Drain

The Flood and Drain is a much simpler design and highly recommended for beginners. There are a number of ways you can approach the design with either a standpipe in the grow bed itself with a timer on the pump or a siphon in the grow bed. There is no definite answer on which is better. They each carry their own advantages and disadvantages. It really comes down to your own preference and whichever is easiest or most accessible to you.

The advantages of this system are the simple design, with only two major system components required. It can be great for those who have taller fish tanks. The disadvantage, however, is the fact that the pump is present in the fish tank and the water level in the tank does fluctuate throughout the process.

Constant Flood

The Constant Flood system is quite similar to the Simple Flood and Drain. The only different being that when the timer is removed from the Simple Flood and Drain, the grow-main remains constantly flooded. The setup is entirely the same as a Simple Flood and Drain, but rather than draining the grow bed, you want to keep the grow bed saturated. The advantages and disadvantages are quite closely connected.

Chapter 3: How To Design Your Own Aquaponics System

Key Takeaway: Setting up your own system is quite simple and can be done with materials purchased at your local hardware or gardening store. The media bed system is simpler and suited for DIY aquaponics farmers, making it a great starting point for beginners in aquaponics.

For our example system design, we will be looking into building one of the simpler methods of aquaponics: the Media Bed also known as the Ebb-and-Flow system.

If you remember from the last chapter, the media bed method consists of a grow bed filled with hydroponic media consisting of clay, pebbles or gravel, along with a fish tank. Using just these two main components, the system is able to flow from the fish tank into the grow bed. This allows the nutrients to be absorbed by the plants and bacteria, cleansing the effluent. This revitalized water is then drawn back into the fish tank through the pump, where it provides clean water and oxygen for the fish.

Components of the Media Bed Aquaponic System

Media Bed

You are able to make a media bed from a number of materials such as plastic, fiberglass or a wooden frame, as long as it is sealed with water-tight rubber or polyethylene sheeting for the base and interior walls. Most people who design their media bed system from scratch use plastic contains, modified IBCs or even old converted bathtubs. Regardless of what you ultimately use for the construction of your media beds, there are criteria that must be followed to ensure that the containers will be able to function correctly as a media bed. These are:

1. Have enough strength to hold water as well the growth media without collapsing;
2. Be averse to weathering conditions for long periods of time;
3. Be made of a material that is safe for the fish, plants and bacteria;
4. Easily connectable to the other unit components using simple plumbing parts; and
5. Can be placed within close proximity to other unit components.

The shape of your media beds is ideally rectangular with a width of around 1 meter and 1-3 meters in length. While you are welcome to use beds that are much larger than this, they do require further support such as concrete blocks in order to hold their weight. If you decide to use longer beds, be aware that this can cause an unequal distribution of the solid wastes, which tend to accumulate at the water inlet which can raise the risk of anaerobic spots.

The depth of your media bed is another important factor to consider as this determines the level of root space volume available, which in turn will determine the types of vegetables that will be available for you to grow. For example, if you are hoping to grow large fruiting vegetables such as tomatoes, okra or cabbage, it is recommended that the media bed you are using has a depth of at least 12 inches. This allows the vegetables to stretch out their roots, avoiding roots matting and maximizing the nutrients that they are able to absorb, as well as keep the plant stabilized in the media bed.

Medium

In order for your medium to allow for a sufficient flow of water and air to allow the bacteria to flourish and the plants roots to breath, you will need to ensure you have adequate space to create enough surface area. For similar reasons, it is best for the medium to be comprised of nontoxic material and a balanced pH level to avoid contaminating the water. It is recommended that, prior to placing the medium into the beds, you wash the surface thoroughly to clean out any materials, such as dust particles and other pieces of gravel, that could cause damage to the system by clogging or causing harm to the fish.

Decide on a medium that you feel comfortable working with. There are many materials that are available to you, such as volcanic gravel (which is the most used), light expanded clay aggregate, river-bed gravel or pumice. There are other materials that can be used, such as organic substrates. While these are inexpensive, they do hold the risk of deteriorating over time, thereby causing damage to the system. If you do choose an organic substrate, it is recommended that you monitor the lifespan of the material and remove and replace it from the system once it begins to break down.

Filtration

The advantage of using a Media Bed Aquatic system is that the medium itself acts as a filter in both a mechanical and biological sense. In order to maximize the efficiency of your system you will need to ensure that the media bed is the right size for the density of your stocked medium. If not, this can cause solids to clog in the system and ultimately lead to poor water circulation. This increases the risk that the toxicity of the water will cause harm to the aquatic life.

You are welcome to also include a solids capture mechanism in your design. If you prefer to design a mechanical filter to compliment your system yet want to stick to a budget, there is a cost-effective technique that you can use with just an old single sock. Attach the sock to where the water from the fish tank flows into the media bed at the tap. Ensure that you maintain the sock each day by removing and rising out the deposited material.

Irrigation System

There are a number of ways for your system to harness the water and drive it to your media beds. Deciding on which technique works for you depends on the materials you have available to you and your personal experience or preferences. The simplest of which can be just placing holes in the pipes that are distributed through your medium, a cost effective and easy to build design.

The flood-and-drain technique, or ebb-and-flow as it is also known, is used to flood the grow beds with the water directly from the fish tank, only to dispose of the excess through the sump tank, allowing the plants to capture the nutrient rich waters in the process. This is a more complex and comprehensive design. In order to construct this design, you will need make use of auto-siphons or timed pump. The advantages of adopting this technique in your design is that it allows the bed to remain constantly in a state of moisture, providing optimal conditions for the bacteria to thrive.

Constructing Your Media Bed Aquaponic System

In order to get started constructing your media bed, you will need a few materials.

Preparing Your Fish Tank

Your first step towards building the media bed is to take your IBC tank and remove the two horizon steel lengths that line the top surface of the container. This can be done by removing the screws (4 star headed) using a star headed screwdriver or key. From there, you will need to remove the inner plastic tank and start drawing up a square shape across the surface of the tank measuring around 2 inches from each of the four sides of the tank. In order to remove the plastic, it is recommended that you use an angle grinder to cut along the lining you have drawn. The removed piece can later be utilized as a cover for your fish tank.

The next step is to wash the inside of the container using soap and warm water. This will help eliminate any containments that are present in the container which can affect the health of the water that circulates through the system.

Installing the Fish Tank Pipe

The next step is to make room for the piping that will connect your media beds to the fish tank for water to flow through. On one side of your IBC tank, mark out a point that measures around 5 inches from the top and 5 inches from the side of the tank. You will then need to drill with a 2.5 inches circular drill bit on that point. Next, you will need to insert a 2 inches wide uniseal along the inside of the hole you had just drilled.

The pipe used to connect the fish tank is comprised of 2 pieces of PVC pipe measuring 2 inches, as well as an elbow piece and coupler of the same measurement. Make horizontal slits using an angle grinder at 1 inch wide along the length of pipe that rests at the bottom surface of the fish tank. This helps waste move through the pipe while keeping the fish in the tank.

Next, you are to seal the open end of the PVC surface pipe with a PVC endcap or stopper that measures 2 inches. A short length of PVC pipe of 2 inches is then slotted through the uniseal, attached to the PVC elbow on the inside end of the tank, and attached to the vertical piping to the other end of the elbow connected to the uniseal.

The final step is then to drill a 0.1 inch hole into the PVC elbow and attach this to the uniseal. This prevents air seals from forming inside the pipe, and draining the water from the fish tank if the pump was to fail due to power outage. Keep in mind this is incredibly important for the protection of your aquatic life, in the event that something goes wrong.

Preparing the Media Beds and Sump Tank

Now that you have your fish tank connected through piping to the media beds, it is time to prepare the sump tank. This will allow water to be drained from the media beds to be recirculated back into the fish tank. In this example, we are building 3 media beds supported by a single sump tank. We will be using our remaining IBC tanks to create the sump tank. One of the media beds from one IBC tank and the second to create the other two media beds. The process will be much the same as step one, by removing the steel profiles and separate the plastic containers.

Turning One IBC into Two Media Beds

By standing the inner plastic container upright, mark out using a leveler and a pencil two bisecting lines 12 inches from both sides of the tank. You will then take an angle grinder to cut along both the lines, allowing you to create two containers each with a depth of 12 inches. As before, ensure that the containers are washed using soap and warm water and left to dry in the sun for 24 hours to prevent containments from entering your system.

Supporting Frame

Building your metal support frame is made simple using the IBC exterior metal frame that you had cut out earlier. Ensure the measurements match up by using the same bisecting lines cut through the plastic using the angle grinder. It is well worth keeping the two horizontal profiles in order to use them to support the sides of your beds once they are in operation to keep them stable.

The support frames are then to be laid out with 6 lengths of wood with four being 41 inches, one of 17 inches and one of 17 inches placed over the frames. This to ensure that the media bed remains in a horizontal shape and keeps the bell siphons functioning correctly. To secure the media beds, place them on top of the support frame, resting on the wood panels using the remaining wood panels to slot in between the plastic media bed and the support frame to enhance the stability.

Building the Sump Tank

With the final IBC container, follow the same process of marking out a single 12 inches bisecting line and using the angle grinder to cut out the plastic container and mental frame. This 12 inches container is then removed. The remaining piece will comprise your sump tank being of 28 inches depth. Once again, ensure that both containers are washed thoroughly using soap and laid out to dry for 24 hours.

From there, we prepare the third media bed using the same steps with wooden lengths of similar specifications as the two previous media beds. The difference here is that a conical drill is used to create holes, which will later house drainage pipes.

Preparing the Bell Siphons

Before we get started making the siphons, you will need to gather some materials to use in the process. In total you will need to make 3 siphons. Each siphon requires the following materials:

- 18 inches media guard (4.3 inches PVC pipe)
- 11 inches bell [PVC pipe (3 inches) with flared end + endcap/stopper (3 inches) + rubber washer (3 inches)]
- 6 inches standpipe (1 inch PVC pipe)
- Barrel connector (1 inch)
- PVC reducer (1 inch)
- PVC female adaptor (1 inch × 1 inch)
- PVC elbow (1 inch × 1 inch female)

The bell is the first step. This is created using a 11 inches piece of PVC (3 inches), which is then cut into two separate pieces. A hole will need to be drilled of 4 inches in each of the two pieces, which are then sealed at one end using a PVC endcap and rubber washer.

The next step is to build the media guards using 18 inches of PVC pipe (110mm), cutting 0.2 inches slots along the length. Each of your media beds will need to have the center points marked out. This can be done in the center of the two wooden panels, where you will be drilling a 1 inch hole in each point and inserting a barrel connector (1 inch) with a rubber washed inside the media bed.

By screwing the PVC adaptor onto the barrel, connecting and slotting the standpoint into the PVC adaptor as well as the second PVC adaptor to the top of the standpoint, you are able to allow a larger volume of water to come through as the tank is filled assisting the siphon in the draining process.

The next step is to place the bell siphons and media guards over the standpipes and allow the water to flow out of the media bed, by connecting the PVC elbow to the other end of the barrel connector.

Assembly

It is now time to assemble your media beds and sump tank. This is done by bracing the sump tank, using cinderblocks along each side, avoiding covering any holes drilled into the tank. Raise the fish tank to around 6 inches from the ground, using blocks, and placing it 4 inches from another set of blocks, which is to be placed 16 inches from the blocks supporting the sump tank.

Assembling the Plumbing

Connecting up the plumbing requires the following parts:

- Barrel connector, B-type (1 inch) × 3
- PVC tap (1 inch) × 3
- PVC endcap/stopper (2 inches) × 3
- PVC elbow (2 inches) × 2
- PVC connector, T (2 inches) × 2
- PVC coupler (2 inches) × 3

- 59 inches of PVC pipe (2 inches) × 1
- 13 inches of PVC pipe (2 inches) × 1

Taking the previous length of PVC (2 inches) that had been slotted through the uniseal in the fish tank, connect a PVC elbow of 2 inches to this pipe. Using a PVC straight couple (2 inches) connect another PVC elbow to connect to this distribution pipe, being the same height as the top of media bed.

In order to create a valve to control the water flow in each of the media beds, take a PVC endcap and drill a 1 inch diameter hold. Insert a barrel connector into the hole, tighten it and then wrap Teflon tape around the threads of the male end of the barrel connector, screwing the tap valve onto the end. Do this a total of three times, one for each media bed.

Allow the water to flow into each of the media beds by attaching pipes from the PVC elbow attached to the fish exit pipe to the sump tank. Next, connect up each media bed using pipe caps fitted with valves to the PVC

T connectors and elbow connects from the distribution pipe.

Media Beds to Sump Tank

Connect a drain pipe of 24 inches length and 1 inch diameter to the elbow connection resting under the media bed and exiting from the bottom of the bell siphon standpipe. Take the pipe and slot it into the easiest available hole drilled on the side of the sump tank, to allow the water to have a clear route to flow through into the sump. Connect the next two media beds using a PVC elbow connect to the end of the barrel connector. You will need to attach 6.4 feet of a 10 inches wide pipe to the drilled holes of the sump tank to connect the furthest media bed and a length of 3.2 feet pipe for the closest.

Sump Tank to the Fish Tank

Connect the pump to be submerged with a piece of a 1 inch pipe, using a straight connector. Then take another length of pipe which will stretch to the inside of the finish tank from the pump in the sump tank. Take this length of pipe and connect it to the top of the fish tank using as little connectors as possible, to ensure that the pump will be of maximum efficiency.

Adding the Medium and Getting Started

Your system should now be ready to start running and circulating the water. It is now time to add the growing medium into the beds. Fill the fish tank and sump tank to double check there are no leaks before adding the medium. If everything is running smoothly, use your chosen medium to stock the beds.

Chapter 4: How To Stock Your Aquaponics System

Key Takeaway: Different types of fish are suited to different environments in terms of climate and water temperature. When you are stocking your tank, ensure that the plants you decide to grow are compatible with the fish that will be in your tank, to avoid mismatching and limiting your yield. Research thoroughly into the plants you are growing, their preferences for climate, and then stock fish to match with similar preferences.

With your system up and running, the next step is to stock the aquatic life and decide on the plats that you will be growing. When considering which plants and fish will be living in your system, you will need to ensure that they are compatible with the temperature and pH level of the system. Having the right balance, with the right fish to grow the right kind of plants, will give you a greater measure of success and require less maintenance down the line.

Some types of fish are more suited for colder climate while others prefer hotter climates. This is something you will need to consider before stocking a particular type of fish. In some cases, you might like to consume your fish. For this reason you might have a preference of edible fish to harvest once the stocks are plentiful.

Fish Species

White Bass

Measuring around 9 inches long, the white bass is a common fish for aquaponics systems. It is a popular choice, if you plan on harvesting fish for consumption. The white bass eats smaller fish, as well as crabs.

Catfish

Another popular choice for aquaponics farmers, the catfish is also highly recommended if you plan on eating fish.

Trout

Trout are more suitable for cold water so it is best to stock these fish either in colder winter times if you live in a climate that experiences warmer seasons, or all year round for colder climate locations. Keep in mind, if you do choose to keep trout in your aquaponics system, you will be limited in the plants that you are able to grow, since many prefer warmer waters.

Goldfish

The popular goldfish is one which you are not able to cook and eat. But they are a good choice for the aquaponics system in that they are resilient in many different water conditions, although they do prefer warmer climates, being tropical fish.

Crappies

Highly recommended for aquaponics, Crappies are well suited to many conditions in your tank. They also make a great meal when cooked. Crappies generally feast on crabs and insects.

Barramundi

Suited to the warmer climates, Barramundi's are great for seasonal harvest in the warmer summer months and then to be feasted on when it gets colder.

Coi

A beautiful ornamental fish, Coi are great for the type of environment that your aquaponics system will present. While they cannot be eaten, they make an excellent decoration for your tank.

Tilapia

Another fish suited for warmer climates, Tilapias is the most popular choice for aquaponics farms in that they are low maintenance, easy to grow and taste great.

Plants to Stock

As previously mentioned, the type of fish you will be keeping in your tank will depend on the temperature and pH level of the water which will be circulating through the system. This ultimately determines the types of plants you will be able to grow, with each having its own set of suited conditions to thrive and provide you with a faster turnaround. The plants you grow provide an excellent, self-sustaining source of food. Through aquaponics, you can grow almost any plant that you would through normal gardening. There are certain plants, however, that are particularly easy to grow, maintain and harvest through aquaponics.

Different plants are also suited for different Aquaponic systems. For example, leafy greens such as lettuce and other herbs are better suited to the floating raft style beds, due to their root structure. Other vegetables are suited towards wicking beds. Tomatoes, peppers beans and most other multiple yield plants are more suited towards media beds.

It is also important to consider the environment you are planting in such as:

- the exposure to sunlight
- the overall temperature of the climate
- rainfall, and
- wind

All need to be taken into account, if you are planning on growing outdoors. In order to have the greatest success rate, it is best to plant according to the seasons, with the colder climate vegetables grown in winter and warmer plants grown in the summer months.

If you are planning on using your hydroponics system as a reliable source of food supply, staggering your harvests is the best way to ensure that you are not collecting all the yields at once and instead can harvest and consume them when they are ripe, avoiding any spoilage. This can take a little bit of practice to get the right timing, but it is all part of the enjoyment of aquaponics farming.

Remember to have some variety in your crops, by growing a diverse range of vegetables over the same period of time. If you do end up with more vegetables than you can consume, you may want to consider donating or giving them away to friends and neighbors. You can also freeze or dehydrate them for later consumption.

Lettuce

If you are hoping for a fast turnaround in yield, lettuce is the best place to start. Each head of lettuce can grow to maturity within around a month. It has a very low maintenance and isn't too fussy in regards to water temperature and the climate that surrounds it.

Tomatoes

If you have a bit more time and patience, tomatoes are another excellent fruit to grow. Taking around three months to mature, they are easily grown in the media bed and prefer a temperature of around 59-95 degrees Fahrenheit.

Carrots

If the climate is right, carrots can make a valued addition to your vegetable garden preferring to be grown at around 50-65 degrees Fahrenheit and taking 65 days to mature for harvest.

Wax bean

Growing an Italian-style wax bean is great for providing you with a food source that is both easily stored and lasts for a long amount of time. It is also highly nutritious. It can take around 54 days for the bean to be harvested. They thrive in temperatures of around 59-95 degrees Fahrenheit, making them quite easy to grow in a variety of conditions.

Other fruits and vegetables

In addition to these vegetables there are numerous other fruits and vegetables that can enhance your garden and provide you with an abundant food source. Herbs in particular such as basil and low-water thyme, are quite easy to grow and can be used a variety of dishes with both your fish and other vegetables in your garden. Other plants that work well in the media beds of an Aquaponic system are strawberries and peppers, adding some color amongst the leafy greens.

Unfortunately, not all plants are suited for the aquaponics style of farming. Some plants prefer pH levels that may be a lot higher or lower than the neutral 7.0. This can make it difficult for them to grow effectively or survive in the environment. For example, blueberries and azaleas thrive in conditions of acidic soil with a lower pH level than what is standard. On the opposite end of the spectrum, chrysanthemums, calendula and zinnias are more suited to soils with a much higher pH level.

If you would like your garden to look more vibrant and add some decorations, some people who have a home-grown aquaponics system also grow certain types of flowers to add some color. Virtually any flower is well suited to an aquaponics environment so it is all down to your personal preference on how you would like to dress up your system.

Chapter 5: How To Maintain Your Aquaponics System

Key Takeaway: Regular maintenance of your system will allow you to avoid extra expenses, which can occur when larger repair jobs are required. When you take into account the fact that your aquaponics system largely maintains itself, the advantages over traditional gardening are still quite clear. By taking care of the fish in your system, the water they live in and the plants that are sustained through nutrients, you are able to keep your system in a condition that allows you to reap the benefits of aquaponics for many years to come, provided you take on the small tasks towards maintaining the system and keeping the conditions optimal.

While aquaponics systems require very little maintenance compared to traditional forms of gardening which require weeding, water and fertilizing, there is still work to be done to ensure that your system is running at optimal efficiency and that you don't have to perform any major work down the line. Maintenance of your aquaponics systems involves frequent checkups and tasks to keep everything working. These can be each day, every week and monthly depending on what you are working to maintain. Without the proper maintenance in place, the system can fall into a state of disrepair and require intervention much sooner than the simple, frequent maintenance tasks that are recommended for taking care of your system.

Daily Activities

Feeding Your Fish

The fish are the life blood of your aquaponics system. Without them, the system would falter and the plants will no longer receive the vital nutrient rich water that the fish provide. It is therefore necessary that your fish are fed well at least once or twice daily, to ensure they are well nourished and continue to thrive in the waters.

Depending on your budget and the time constraints you have on your system, you may want to invest in an automatic fish feed to allow the fish to receive regular doses of food if you are unable to commit to feeding them each day. Although if you are actively engaged with your aquaponics system and continue to address maintenance issues each day and week, feeding your fish is a small task that will allow you to also check the tank for any larger issues that could be present and grow larger in time.

Checking the Water Temperature

Maintaining the correct water temperature is not only beneficial for the fish in your tank, it also helps ensure that the particular plants you are growing are compatible with the water. If the water temperature fluctuates regularly and needs external influence, checking the water temperature daily provides you with an opportunity to do this before any further damage is done on behalf of your fish or the plants growing.

Weekly Activities

Monitor for Insects

Unfortunately, even with aquaponics, your plants risk being consumed by insects. This is where it is helpful to perform regular checks on the plants, to ensure that a small insect problem doesn't manifest into something more destructive that can lead to the loss of your plant life. Checking for insects involves checking the leaves of the plants, as well as along the streams of water and removing any evidence of insects invading the system.

Checking the pH Levels

Keep in mind that both the plants, fish and the bacteria living in your system all depend on having a particular pH level for them to thrive and enjoy the nutrients provided. Without the correct pH level in place, the entire system can fall into chaos and ultimately destroy not just your plant harvest but also the fish living in the tank. It is recommended that you check the pH level of your system at least once a week and monitor a reading between 6.8 and 7.0. In most cases the aquaponics system will regulate the pH level independently.

However, it does naturally decline over time, and this is where maintenance is required. Increasing the pH level is as simple as adding hydrated lime or potash to the fish tank.

Check the Ammonia Levels

Your aquaponics system generally requires ammonia levels of 0.5ppm or less to maintain optimal health. It is recommended that the ammonia levels are checked on a weekly basis, to ensure that there are no fish that have died in your tank, driving up the ammonia levels in the system and causing issues to the health of your plant life and other fish.

Monthly Activities

Check the Nitrate levels

Maintaining nitrate levels ensures that your plants are receiving the correct amount of nutrients to survive and grow into a healthy harvest. In some cases, the nitrate levels may rise to abnormally high levels of above 150ppm. This is where maintenance is required to bring those levels down.

There are a number of ways by which the quality of your system can be improved, such as:

- removing some of the fish for harvest
- growing more plants, or
- adding another grow bed to expand your aquaponics system (in cases where the nitrate levels are quite high).

Nitrate levels aren't too much a cause for concern. Therefore, it is recommended that they are checked monthly, in case the level of fish have increased, or you harvested some of the plants.

Check Pumps and Plumbing System

A system that has experienced failed pumps or plumbing is a system that is no longer working as it should. This can cause a myriad of issues, including the entire failure of your system. Therefore, it is important to regularly maintain the plumbing and pumping equipment to avoid this occurring. It is recommended that you check the system each day briefly, to ensure that everything is running smoothly to reduce the risk of failure occurring. Monthly maintenance of this equipment is also recommended. This involves cleaning out the pipes, using a high-pressure hose to free any sediments that can cause blockages and damage to the pump.

Chapter 6: How to Pick The Best Location For Your Aquaponics System

__Key Takeaway__: Deciding on a location means you need to take into consideration many factors to get the most out of your system and avoid hassle later on. Not everyone has room in their backyard for an aquaponics system, so ensure that you can take into account as many of these factors as possible to make aquaponics an effortless operation, providing benefits for many years to come.

Where you place your aquaponics system is highly important to the long-term success of the operation. Having the system placed in the right location means you will need to consider:

- the amount of sunlight the system receives
- the water source available
- the electrical source to keep the pump working, and
- the temperature source to maintain consistent temperature in the water for both the fish and the plants you are growing.

You will also need to ensure that the exhaust fans from the electronic pump are facing away from the home, to avoid having toxic gases in the vicinity of your home and your family, which can cause health issues over time.

Space

The first consideration for your aquaponics location is the surrounding space. Not everyone has a backyard to house an aquaponics system. This is where you need to make comprises. If you are planning on accessing both water and electricity from the house, you will need to make sure the houses and wires are run from a small distance and do not take up too much room in your garden or cause any hazards when they are in operation.

You will also want to ensure that your system has plenty of space around the perimeter, to ensure that you are able to easily access the system for planting, harvesting and maintenance. This includes both the grow beds and the fish tank, as you will need an easy access point to reach into the system for either maintaining or harvesting both the plants and fish.

Having a system located in a corner, while it may be out of the way, can also mean you will have more difficulty accessing the tanks and grow beds putting yourself at risk of injury. With some plants growing over the edge of the grow beds, you will also want to leave room for them to expand and therefore spacing the grow beds out by 28 inches will provide adequate space for growth.

It is also best to avoid placing your system close by trees, particularly deciduous trees which can shed leaves, flowers or other debris that can land in your tank. This can add extra maintenance work and may even place your fish at risk of toxicity. Having a cover over system which allows for sunlight to reach both the plants and the fish, will ideally avoid any debris from entering the system and contaminating the water.

Sunlight

Ideally, your plants and fish will receive a good amount of sunlight during the day. This means you need to take into account where the system is located in terms of shading from trees and buildings which can block sunlight, reducing the rate of exposure during the day. Your system will need at least 6 hours of sunlight each day. Some growers prefer to keep their aquaponics system inside a greenhouse. This will provide both amble sunlight and keep the heat stored in the atmosphere, thus creating an ideal environment for the plants.

The fish tank, however, is better suited to avoid direct sunlight, as this can cause algae blooms and affect the health of the fish by reducing the availability of oxygen in the tank. In order to ensure that the plants receive optimal sunlight, while also keeping the fish out of direct sunlight, consider placing a cover of your fish tank to create some shade as well as placing some float plants on the surface of the water, which can provide your fish with shelter and a place to avoid the sun.

Proximity to Your Home

An ideal location for your aquaponics system outside of a greenhouse is located within close proximity to your house, ideally along a south facing wall. This will allow your system to have access to both electricity and water, as well as heat which is absorbed from the house, reflected back onto the aquaponics system. This will also prevent any unsightly wires or hoses running from the house and across the lawn, as they will much easier connect from the house.

Heating and Insulation

In order to ensure that your water temperature is ideal for the growth of the fish and the bacteria growing within your system, you may want to consider a submersible heater to regulate the temperature. This does depend on the type of fish that you have in your tank and their preference of heat, but is also an important consideration if your local climate is prone to fluctuations that can place the fish at risk of stunting their growth or dying off altogether.

Storing Equipment

You will find in the process of building and maintaining your system that aquaponics comes with a lot of accessories and supplies that come with the process of being an aquaponics farmer. For this reason, you will want to have a place to store things in a place that allows you to have easy access. Pipes, tubes, cables, fish supplies and gardening tools will all need to be stored close to your aquaponics system, for regular maintenance and whenever your system needs intervention. This could be as simple as a garden shed. Or perhaps you would even like to go as far as building your own storage location. Either way, it is important to consider where you will be storing these items when choosing a location for your aquaponics system.

Safety

The final consideration when deciding on a location for your system is safety. If you happen to have young children and pets on your property, you will need to ensure your aquaponics system is set up and located in a space that will be out of harm's way for any children or pets to either accidently damage the system or injure themselves in some way. This can be done as simply as putting up a barrier or fence around the system, or placing it in a way that will prevent children from climbing over the system or having access to the equipment.

Conclusion

Thanks again for taking the time to read this book!

You should now have a firm understanding of the nature of aquaponics. Remember that aquaponics is the marriage of both aquaculture and hydroponics. The benefits of aquaponics should now be quite evident, as well as how aquaponics is changing the shape of farming in both plants for food as well as fish. Aquaponics holds many benefits over traditional farming in that once the system is established there is very little work involved in maintaining that system and harvesting the yield. The hydroponic aspect also holds many benefits of standard aquaponics, with many of the harmful and expensive chemicals used in the hydroponic process being replaced by the effluent rich waters produced by the fish your system.

If you want to learn more about Hydroponics, check out my book *'Hydroponics 101: The Easy Beginner's*

Guide to Hydroponic Gardening. Learn How To Build a Backyard Hydroponics System for Homegrown Organic Fruit, Herbs and Vegetables.'

You have also learned how the system works, with the fish consuming food and producing the effluent rich waters, which is then converted into nitrate by the bacteria living in the water. The water then flows into the grow beds through a number of different methods. From there, the water is drained into the sump tank to carry the oxygenated water back into the fish tank, to provide the fish with oxygen now that the effluent has been removed by the plants.

The basics of building your own backyard system was outlined in chapter three, detailing the materials that you are able to purchase from a basic gardening or hardware store which can be easily assembled to create your own aquaponics system. While we only explored one of the simpler systems to build, you are welcome to explore other options which are slightly more intricate if you want to attain certain benefits, or grow certain vegetables that are better suited to the other methods of aquaponics.

Learning which fish and plants to grow was outlined in chapter four, to help you decide on the best combination. Some fish do prefer either warmer or colder waters. There are plants that have their preference as well. Taking into account the climate you live in will help you decide whether to invest in a water heater or whether your fish and plants will coexist and thrive naturally without interference.

Maintaining your system is much more passive than traditional gardens, which is one of the great benefits of having an aquaponics system. In chapter five, you learned the basic activities you will do daily, weekly and monthly to keep your aquaponics system in optimal shape and to avoid anything going wrong and affecting the health of your fish and plants.

In the final chapter, we explored the considerations that need to be made in regards to where you will need to locate your system, taking into account sunlight, the surrounding space, the temperature and the distance from the house. It is not always easy to find a particular spot that will be perfect for establishing your system but the more considerations you make, the better the chances your system will produce a maximum yield and require less oversight.

Your aquaponics journey is just beginning. There is an entire wealth of knowledge worth exploring into this hobby and seeing how far you can take it. From here you can create your own self-sustaining food source.

Be sure to do further research and keep your options open. Because what kinds of fish you can stock and what kinds of plants you can grow in your system ultimately depends on how vivid your imagination and inner desires are.

BONUS CHAPTER: What is Hydroponics?

*This is a bonus chapter from my book '**Hydroponics 101**: The Easy Beginner's Guide to Hydroponic Gardening. Learn How To Build a Backyard Hydroponics System for Homegrown Organic Fruit, Herbs and Vegetables.'*

Enjoy!

***

***Key Takeaway**: Hydroponics is the art of growing plants without soil.*

So, you want to give hydroponic growing of plants a try. Wonderful! But what exactly is hydroponics?

Hydroponics Explained

Hydroponics is the art of growing plants without soil. The word "Hydroponic" actually means "working water" in Latin. There are many methods of hydroponic gardening. The plants can be grown in gravel, liquid, or sand. Nutrients can be added, but the key thing to remember is that the plants are grown without soil.

Why Grow Plants Without Soil?

The first thing you need to understand is why plants "require" soil in the first place.

Soil is important to the growing and nurturing of plants because the soil acts as a medium for growth. A medium for growth is simply the substance that bears the weight of the plant and keeps it upright while the root system does its job. The soil is able to store the required nutrients the plant needs, and it serves as a mode for balancing normal pH levels in the roots of the plant.

If the pH levels in the plant's roots are unstable, it begins to break down the roots which can inhibit the plant's ability to absorb the required minerals it needs to thrive. This imbalance is one of the highest causes of plant death among those attempting to flex their green thumb, and it is what causes many individuals to give up.

However, when you give a plant what it needs when it needs, in the amount it requires, the plant can thrive no matter what its roots are submerged in.

In hydroponics, that medium for growth is water, and the nutrients come from carefully measured and organically-produced products that are combined with the plant's water source.

With hydroponics, the roots are given a break. In soil, the roots have to branch out and search for the nutrients, which is how all plants obtain their soiled root systems. In water, the dissolved proportion of nutrients do not have to be sought out, and the energy that is usually expended developing the roots is now spent developing the plant itself, which can aid in the speed in which the plant grows and produces fruits and vegetables.

There are six basic systems in hydroponics. We will discuss those next.

***

This is the end of this bonus chapter.

Want to continue reading?

Then go to the Amazon website and search for "Hydroponics 101."

Hope to see you there!

Did You Like This Book?

If you enjoyed this book, I would like to ask you for a favor. Would you be kind enough to share your thoughts and post a review of this book on Amazon? Just a few sentences would already be really helpful.

You can simply find it by:

- searching for 'Aquaponics 101' on Amazon, or
- checking your purchases on your Amazon account.

Your voice is important for this book to reach as many people as possible.

The more reviews this book gets, the more people will be able to find it and learn how they can grow their own organic vegetables with aquaponics.

Thank you again for reading this book and good luck with applying everything you have learned!

I'm rooting for you...

By The Same Author

CBD

HEMP OIL 101

The Essential Beginner's Guide To CBD & Hemp Oil to Improve
Health, Reduce Pain and Anxiety, and Cure Illnesses

TOMMY ROSENTHAL

DIY
CANNABIS
EXTRACTS
101

The Essential And Easy Beginner's Cannabis Cookbook
On How To Make Medical Marijuana Extracts At Home

TOMMY ROSENTHAL

Notes

CPSIA information can be obtained
at www.ICGtesting.com
Printed in the USA
LVHW081250180422
716523LV00019B/192